First published in Great Britain 1978 by Colour Library International Ltd.
© Illustrations reproduced by courtesy of the Museum del Prado, Madrid (Salmer, Archivo Fotografico, Barcelona).
Colour separations by La Cromolito, Milan, Italy.
Display and text filmsetting by Focus Photoset, London, England.
Printed and bound by L.E.G.O. Vicenza, Italy.
ISBN 0 904681 88 2
**COLOUR LIBRARY INTERNATIONAL**

…scape with the Embarkation …Paula of Rome at Ostia' *right* …cal of the work of the …h artist Claude **Lorrain** …0-1682).

…kating Scene', the only …osition by Joost Cornelisz **…chsloot** (c. 1586-1666) … is owned by The Prado.

…'A Harbour' by Johannes **…llis** (c. 1548-1632) is also the …representation of this artist's …in the Gallery.

*…left* is a typical scene of rustic …y by David **Teniers** the …ger which is entitled 'A …try Fete'.

*…af* 'The Holy Family' by **…ael** is known as 'The Pearl' …as formerly in the …ssion of King Philip IV.

*Below far left* is 'The Money Changer and his Wife' by Marinus **van Reymerswaele** (c. 1500–1567). The picture is dated 1539 and was bequeathed to The Prado in 1934.

Anton **van Dyck** (c. 1599–1641) was a pupil of Rubens and is regarded as one of the world's finest portrait painters. His 'Portrait of Frederick Henry de Nassau, Prince of Orange' *left* is a particularly fine example. 'St Barbara' *below left* is a wing of a triptych by the **Master of Flémalle** depicting St Barbara in the tower where she was imprisoned by her father.

*Right* is the only painting in the Prado by J. D. **Cooseman**: 'Still Life with a Tray of Fruit'.

*Below* is 'A Larder' by Adriaen van **Utrecht** (c. 1599–1652), the prominent Flemish painter.

Few artists have painted so many self portraits as Albrecht **Dürer** (c. 1471–1528). The Prado portrait *left* is one of Dürer's most important works.

'Moses saved from the Waters of
the Nile' *above* is a small canvas b
**Veronese.**

'Portrait of a Lady Revealing her
Breast' *above left* by Jacopo Robus
commonly known as **Tintoretto**
(c. 1518-1594) is one of his most
delicate and beautiful portraits.

Antoine **Watteau's** (c. 1684-1721
delightful and charming
paintings, of which the Prado
owns two: 'Party in a Park' and '*f*
Marriage Contract and Country
Dance' *left*, depicted a fairy-tale
world far removed from the war
and poverty of contemporary
France.

The great Dutch painter,
Harmensz van **Rembrandt**
(c. 1606-1669) was the foremost
member of the 'realist' school of
Holland. His paintings are
remarkable for their light and
shade and he achieved dramatic
effects with his use of colour. H
portrait 'Queen Artemesia' is
shown *right*.

The 16th century painter, Joachim **Patinir** (c. 1480-1524), is considered one of the best of the Flemish landscape painters. Occasionally, however, the magnificent background tends to swamp the theme itself, as in his painting 'Crossing the Styx' *above*.

The paintings by Paolo **Veronese** (c. 1528-1588) are marked by a love of luxury and wealth: rich attire, voluptuous feminine beauty, splendid and majestic architecture, all reflecting the gaiety and power of contemporary Venetian life. A fine example of the artist's work 'Venus and Adonis' is shown *right*.

David **Teniers** the Younger (c. 1610-1690) painted many popular scenes of Dutch working-class life. An example of his work is shown *left*, entitled 'The Kitchen'. *Above left* can be seen 'Smokers and Drinkers' by Adriaen **Brouwer** (c. 1605-1638).

*Above* 'The Finding of Moses' is a mature work by Orazio **Gentileschi** (c. 1565-1639), who was of the Italian school. This picture was painted for Philip IV who employed him at court. In both Gentileschi's work and that of his daughter Artemesia, who was also an artist, the influence of Caravaggio is apparent.

Frans **Snyders** (c. 1579-1657) was responsible for a revival in still-life painting. He was also a great painter of animals and particularly enjoyed painting hunting scenes and illustrations of Aesop's fables. His pictures are Baroque in their form and rich colour. 'The Cook in the Larder' *left* shows his highly-skilled composition and attention to detail. Snyders was an assistant to Rubens and responsible for a number of animals depicted in Rubens' work.

Jacob **Jordaens** (c. 1593-1678) was also a follower of Rubens and often painted epic and mythological subjects. The influence of Rubens is evident in 'The Artist's Family in a Garden' *below* but Jordaens had a greater love of contrasts which make the colours appear especially bright. This splendid picture is regarded as Jordaens' masterpiece.

*ft* 'Meleager and Atalanta' by Jacob **Jordaens** is naturalistic in its treatment and shows a masterly appreciation of solid form in *e* painting of the animals.

Peter Paul **Rubens** (c. 1577-1640) is the most important figure in the art of Flanders and many of his works are owned by the Prado. 'The Three Graces' *above* was painted in 1639. The scene shows the nude figures of Aglaia, Euphrosyne and Thalia. The brilliant use of colour, both in this work and in 'Diana and her Nymphs surprised by Satyrs' *above right*, is apparent. The subtlety, delicacy, and the atmosphere of gaiety in 'The Garden of Love' *overleaf* makes this one of Rubens' finest works.

*Right* is shown 'Venus with an Organist and a small dog' by Tiziano Vecellio, known as **Titian**. Titian was enormously successful and became the favourite painter of both Charles V and Philip II of Spain. His paintings show an excellent blend of colour and mastery in the use of light.

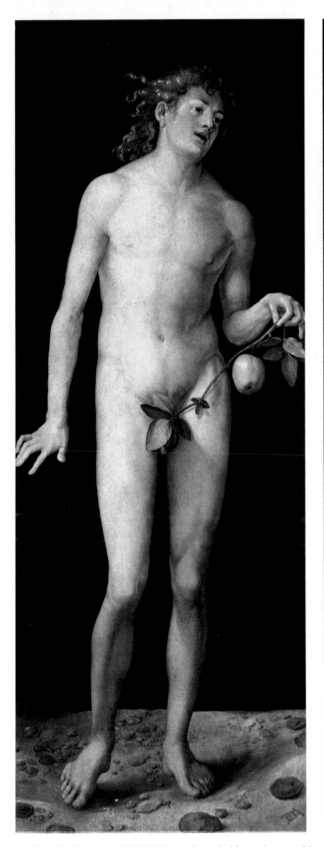

Albrecht **Dürer** (c. 1471-1528) was born in Nuremberg and is noted for his artistic innovations, introducing the nude figure in German art, and 'Adam' and 'Eve' *above* show Dürer at his most effective. The compositions are harmonious, with delicate colouring and detail against a stark background.

*Right* is shown 'The Three Graces' or 'Harmony' by Hans **Baldung Grün** (c. 1484-1545). Grün's nudes are considered to be more elegant and refined than those of Dürer.

The pictures reproduced on these pages are from the Italian school of the 14th and 15th centuries. **Fra Angelico** da Fiesole (c. 1387-1455) was a friar and active painter in the monastery of San Marco in Florence. His art reflects a profound religious feeling. 'The Annunciation' *below left* was painted between 1430 and 1445 and forms part of an altarpiece. Detail from 'The Adoration of the Kings' is shown *left*.

The Prado owns three paintings by the great Italian artist Sandro **Botticelli** (c. 1445-1510). Four panels, three of which are in the Prado and one of which is in a collection in London, were painted under the title 'The Story of Nastagio degli Onesti' which was inspired by a well-known story from Boccacio's 'Decameron'. The three scenes from the panel are shown *above right, right and below.*

**Pieter Bruegel the Elder** (c. 1525-1569) is regarded as the greatest Dutch painter of the 16th century. He is known for his paintings of peasant life. Brueghel, however, also painted nightmarish scenes in the manner of Bosch, such as 'The Triumph of Death' *left* in which the festive Flemish village scene has become frenzied and macabre.

**Jan Brueghel the Elder** (c. 1568–1625) was the son of Pieter Brueghel the Elder. His paintings of velvets and other fine materials earned him the name of 'Velvet Brueghel'. 'The Sense of Taste' *above* is one of a series of paintings by this eminent artist.

*right* 'Landscape with People Walking' is by **Pieter Brueghel the Younger** who lived from (1564-1638), and was another talented member of the Brueghel family.

**Raphael** Santi (c. 1483-1520) is noted for his paintings of the Virgin and Child. 'The Holy Family' *overleaf left* is a beautiful and delicate painting.

*overleaf right* is shown 'Portrait of a Cardinal'.

**Bosch's** triptych, known as 'The Garden of Delights', was originally called 'The Painting of Strawberries' or 'Lust'. Strawberries were considered a symbol of lust and the theme of the work is sensuality and the transience of sexual pleasure. Bosch's world of fantasy and his imaginative use of metamorphosis anticipates the contemporary Surrealist movement.

The right wing of the triptych *above* shows the Creation of Eve in the Garden of Eden, whilst the left wing, illustrated *left*, reveals Hell, symbolising man's punishment. The central panel *right* depicts a world of figures mixed with extraordinary types of vegetation, representative of sensuality and lust, which eventually leads the sinner to eternal damnation.

Very little is known about the life of the eminent Dutch painter of the 15th and 16th centuries, Hieronymus **Bosch** (c. 1450-1516). Highly original, he became known for the nightmarish quality of his paintings and his satirical comments on the folly of man, which he conveyed by the use of symbolism. In the Haywain triptych, the central panel of which is reproduced *left*, the cart of golden hay represents Materialism and the painting includes the most powerful earthly leaders of the time, including the King, the Emperor and the Pope. Pulling the cart are creatures from hell, symbolising sin in all its forms.

*Above* is shown 'The Table of the Seven Deadly Sins'. Christ is depicted in the centre surrounded by the seven deadly sins. Within each of the four circles at the corners is shown Death, Judgement, Hell and Heaven. This picture was a particular favourite of Philip II.

Although not one of the supreme European masters, Rogier van der **Weyden** (c. 1400-1464) is important in the history of art as an artist who popularised Flemish painting. 'The Deposition of Christ' *below* shows the dramatically gesturing figures, emphasised by the gold background, standing almost in the nature of a sculptured relief.

Although Hans **Memling** (c. 1415-1494) was trained by Rogier van der Weyden, an Italian influence can be detected in his work. 'The Adoration of the Magi' *right* is the centre panel of a triptych, the wings of which represent the Nativity and the Presentation of Christ in the Temple. The picture originally belonged to Charles V and adorned the altar of the chapel of the castle of Ateca, near Aranjuez. It was moved to the Prado in 1847.

*Left* is the 'The Cure of Folly' by Hieronymus **Bosch**.

**Greco's** portraits show a touching
implicity, with the features sharply defined
against a neutral background. Of particular
note is the expressiveness of the eyes,
where, it seems, the very soul of the sitter is
captured by this great artist. The influence of
ntoretto is evident in his early work
ortrait of a Gentleman with a Hand at his
east' *below*. The rendition of the hand,
th the second and third finger touching, is
characteristic of El Greco.

'St John the Evangelist' is particularly
arkable for the splendid drapery of the
es. This picture was donated to the
lo in 1921.

Crucifixion with the Virgin, St Mary
dalene, St John the Evangelist and
els' *right* is freely constructed with
gated figures. The realistic detail of
st's dripping blood being wiped away
foot of the cross is typical of El
o's work.

'The Baptism of Christ' *below* is a mature work painted by **El Greco** between 1597 and 1600. This picture skilfully harmonises humanity and divinity.

'The Holy Trinity' *right* was painted about 1577 as the principal part of an altarpiece for the new church of Santo Domingo el Antiguo. It is an early work which still shows Italian influence.

Domenico Theotocopuli, known as **El Greco**
(The Greek), (c. 1541-1614), came to Venice from
his native Crete as a pupil of Titian. By 1577 he
was resident in Spain where his work showed a
Byzantine and Venetian influence, which
culminated in an extraordinary, individual style.
El Greco boldly disregarded the accepted natural
forms and colours, and his work is characterised
by twisted, elongated and ethereal figures. The
pathos of 'San Sebastian' *top left* is markedly
different from the classical concept, the forms and
density of the clouds, and translucent, dark and
mysterious sky giving a profound spirituality to
the work.

The awesome intensity, which is always
apparent in El Greco's religious paintings, is
conveyed in 'The Adoration of the Shepherds'
*right* and 'The Coronation of the Virgin' *left*.
'The Descent of the Holy Ghost' *above* and 'The
Resurrection of Christ' *overleaf left* are late works.

*Right* is 'The Immaculate Conception', a painting of serene beauty with emphasis on warm, golden tones. The sentimentality is characteristic of Murillo's Madonnas, but the Virgin's face conveys, within her simplicity, her glory and divinity.

13

painted with charm and a vigorous realism, using clear yet soft colour. The characterisation of the shepherds in 'The Adoration of the Shepherds' *bottom left* is very natural and human, which tempers the emotional intensity of the subject. Again, despite the religious nature of 'The Holy Family with a Bird' *left*, there is no glorification or sentimentality: the group is depicted as any ordinary family from Seville.

*Below* is shown 'The Virgin Rewarding St Ildefonso for his Writings', and *right* 'The Virgin and St Anne'.

Bartolomé Esteban **Murillo** (c. 1617-1682) was the most prolific and successful representative of the Seville school of painting. His paintings of the Immaculate Conception and the Virgin and Child were particularly esteemed in the 19th century and earned him the title of 'The Spanish Raphael', whilst his real-life subjects were

The picture *left*, 'The Surrender of Breda', was painted by **Velázquez** for the Salón de Reinos, to mark a previous victory when the Dutch General, Justin of Nassau, surrendered the city of Breda to the Spanish forces. Here the Spanish general, Ambrose Spinda, is shown receiving the keys of the fortress from Justin of Nassau.

'The Forge of Vulcan' *below*, which was painted about 1630, shows a mastery of technique that gives a unity to the picture.

*Right* 'The Adoration of the Magi' is another magnificent Velázquez painting on view in the gallery.

*Right* 'Portrait of Prince Baltasar Carlos on Horseback' was painted for the Salón de Reinos in the Buen Retiro Palace and shows a remarkable gravity and calmness of expression in the Prince.

**Velázquez** painted a great many portraits of his King, spanning 37 years. Far from idealising Philip IV however, in every portrait Velázquez brings out the humanity of the King and a certain vulnerability is felt beneath the glory of his attire and pose. The postu of the King in the portrait 'Philip IV on Horseback' *above* is brave, yet Velázquez also conveys a certain lack of aggression. Such frankness in a court painter was unusual and its acceptance by the sitter even more remarkable.

Diego Rodriguez de Silva y **Velázquez** (c. 1599–1660) dominated Spanish painting in the 17th century and is regarded as one of the best painters of all time. His work is characterised by an independence of vision and an outstanding use of colour: he conveys form and texture brilliantly by the use of bold brush strokes. Velázquez was appointed painter to Philip IV in 1623, mainly to portray the King and members of the royal family. His brilliant technique brought out a humanity and naturalism beneath the formality, creating masterpieces of portraiture.

*Below left* 'Portrait of the Cardinal-Infant Don Fernando of Austria' is one of three hunting portraits executed by Velázquez.

*Below* 'Portrait of Pablo de Valladolid', the palace buffoon, was painted about 1633.

*Right* is shown 'Portrait of the Infanta Margaret of Austria'. Velázquez is noted for his remarkable portraits of children.

*Top Left* 'The Spinners' is a brilliant and original painting which demonstrates Velázquez's understanding of perspective and composition.

*Right* is **Goya's** 'Portrait of General Don José de Palafox on Horseback'. Palafox won enormous acclaim for his conduct as Governor of Saragossa during the two sieges of the city by the French in 1808. He was appointed Captain-General of Aragon by Ferdinand VII after the Restoration in 1814 and commanded the King's Guard from 1820-1823. This portrait was painted at the height of Palafox's fame.

*Above*, 'The Snowstorm'. This is the only snow scene that Goya ever painted and is one of thirteen cartoons for tapestries for the dining room of El Prado. Several famous tapestries have since been woven from this painting. The predominance of steel blue in this work emphasises the bleakness and coldness of the scene.

Although described as 'cartoons', **Goya's** productions for the Royal tapestry workshops are, in fact, canvasses. The three which are reproduced here are among the best of the over sixty-three which Goya executed between the ages of twenty-nine and forty-six. These cartoons are original and beautiful works. Goya revolutionised the technique of tapestry work and painted with luminous and vivid colour, producing surprising effects. His cartoons depict the simple pleasures of common life: picnics, games and dances, all in romantic settings. The figures, particularly the women and children, are painted with freshness, grace of movement and delicate modelling of the features. Goya maintains a closeness to nature by his remarkable use of light and colour.

*Left*, 'The Crockery Seller'.
*Below*, 'Blind Man's Buff'.
*Right*, 'The Grape Harvest'.

The suppression of a revolt
by the people in 1808 gave
Goya the inspiration for the
paintings 'The Citizens of
Madrid fighting Murat's
Cavalry 2nd May, 1808' *top
right* and his brilliantly
original 'The Executions of
3rd May, 1808' *right*.

Further paintings illustrating
Goya's mastery are:

*Top left*, 'San Isidro's
Procession'.

*Centre left*, 'The Witches'
Sabbath'; one of a series of
paintings portraying
nightmarish visions.

*left*, 'Two men Fighting with
Clubs'.

Francisco **Goya** (c. 1746-1828) earned a place at the Spa[ni]sh court through his abilities in portraiture. Although it wa[s] in the Spanish tradition to idealise, Goya's depiction of t[he] less attractive aspects of human nature was almost ruthle[ss] in its realism. Perhaps one of the most successful group portraits ever painted, 'The Family of Charles IV of Spain' is shown *right*. 'Portrait of the Duke and Duchess of Osuna and their Children' *top left* is typical of Goya's style, which however, is always elegant and superbly delicate.

The maja's pose in both 'The Naked Maja' and 'The Clothed Maja' *top right* brings to mind Venus, by Velázquez, in 'The Toilet of Venus'. Nudes were prohibited at that time and it is probable that the two paintings were originally kept in a type of double-hinged frame with the clothed picture in front, – the nude only to be revealed on appropriate occasions.

*Left* 'The Hermitage of St Isidor[e] on a Festival Day' was painted b[y] **Goya** in 1788, as a tapestry sket[ch.]

*Above* is shown 'Self-Portrait' b[y] **Goya**, aged about 70.

*Right* 'The Last Supper' by Juan de **Juanes** (c. 1523–1579) shows a perfect composition of figures in the classical style.

*Left* 'St Francis comforted by an Angel playing a lute' is by Francisco **Ribalta** (c. 1565–1628). Ribalta is believed to have trained José **Ribera** (c. 1591–1652) and the gallery contains a number of his works, including 'Jacob's Dream' *below*. Ribera was influenced by Caravaggio, but his paintings are markedly different in that he lacks Caravaggio's subtle structuring.

In contrast to Ribera's liking for often disagreeable realistic detail, Francisco de **Zurbarán** (c. 1598–1664) painted sombre and monumental figures using little shading and with a lack of perspective. This technique, with his fondness for stark and plain backgrounds, is evident in his portrait 'St Casilda' *below right*.

*Below far right* 'The Miracle of the Well' is by Alonso **Cano** (c. 1601–1667) who was a companion of Velázquez. This scene of working-class life illustrates the artist's excellent use of light and shade.

*Below left* is shown the painting by Luis **Paret** y Alcazar (c. 1746-1799), 'Charles III of Spain at Table before his Courtiers'. Paret was renowned for painting scenes of ordinary life – unusual in Spanish painting – and three of his works are owned by the Prado. Another example of his work can be seen *left*, 'The Royal Horse Races'.

A contemporary of Goya, **Bayeu** y Subias (c. 1734-1795), was official painter to the King and produced many fine tapestries for the Madrid tapestry works, including 'The Walk in the Garden of Delights in Madrid' shown *right*.

*Below*. 'The Ascent of a Montgolfier Balloon at Madrid' is by Antonio **Carnicero** who was born in Salamanca in 1748 and died in Madrid in 1814.

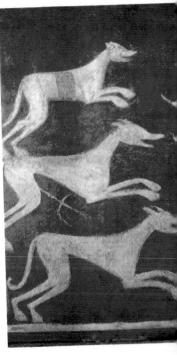

*Left* 'St Dominic of Silos', the central panel of a triptych, was painted by Bartholome **Bermejo** (b. c. 1442). The lavish use of gold is typical of Spanish art of this time. The figures sitting on the throne represent the three virtues – Faith (left), Hope (centre) and Charity (right), and below them, the four cardinal virtues: Justice and Fortitude (left) and Prudence and Temperance (right).

The paintings *above and right* are the work of unknown Spanish artists. 'Hare Hunt' (detail) *above* is a striking example of Spanish Romanesque. It was painted by an artist from Berlanga and is one of a series of pictures on the theme of hunting. The painting *right* is titled 'The Retable of Archbishop Don Sancho de Rojas' containing Madonna and Child scenes. It was painted in the early 15th century and comes from the monastery of San Benito at Valladolid.

# INTRODUCTION

One of the greatest art collections in the world is fittingly housed in the majestic building of the Prado, in the south-eastern part of Madrid. The building itself is impressive as one of the finest examples of Spanish neo-classical architecture and it is delightfully situated with the Botanical Gardens to the south, the church of San Jerónimo to the east and the Buen Retiro Park a very short distance away.

In the grounds of the building stand monuments to some of the great painters whose works are exhibited within: heralding the front with lawns on either side is a large statue of **Velázquez**, to the southern side is a statue of **Murillo** and at the northern façade is a monument to **Goya**.

The gallery has as its base royal collections of various Spanish monarchs and the Spanish School is the best represented of any gallery in the world. The birth of the Prado, however, was a long and laborious process. The building was begun at the order of Charles III in 1787, who commissioned the architect Juan de Villanueva to build a natural history museum. Before its completion the building was war damaged and, on his return to Spain after the War of Independence, Ferdinand VII decided to adapt and restore the building with the intention of forming a picture gallery, by gathering together various paintings which had been dispersed in different buildings by the foreign government. The King personally supervised the restoration of the paintings and arrangements of the rooms and the Picture Gallery was finally opened on 19th November 1819.

During his reign Ferdinand VII continued to work on the building by adding extensions, and various alterations have been undertaken ever since to both the interior and the exterior. In 1956 two new wings were built, adding 15 new rooms. The gallery was subsequently rearranged so that the paintings by the great artists could be kept together in order that a more comprehensive view of the development of each artist's work might be obtained.

When it opened, the gallery contained just over 300 pictures. It has been built up to the vast collection it is today by royal decrees and orders, donations and bequests, and purchases using the gallery's own funds. The treasures amassed by the kings of Spain and the contributions made by the Trinidad museum, however, form by far the most important part of the collection.

The ten generations of sovereigns who were responsible for the formation of the nucleus of the collection showed a fine discrimination in their passion for art and their individual tastes are reflected in the paintings they chose. The Spanish kings were attracted not only by their native art; the gallery owns many important works by other European artists. The Flemish school is particularly well represented, with works by **Bosch**, for whom Philip II had a particular fascination, **Van der Weyden, Rubens** and **Van Dyck**. Philip II admired **Titian** and the gallery therefore owns many of his best portraits. Belonging to the Italian School are excellent works in the gallery by **Veronese, Botticelli, Tintoretto, Fra Angelica** and **Raphael** – masterpieces of vital importance to a comprehensive study of these great artists.

**Velázquez** was private painter to Philip IV, and the Prado therefore owns all his most important works. Also in the collection are outstanding paintings by **Goya** and the gallery has a special exhibition of his collected drawings which is well worth visiting. The Spanish School contains excellent works by **Murillo, El Greco, Ribalta, Morales** and **Ribera**. The Prado is unquestionably one of the greatest art galleries in the world and a knowledge of its collection is essential for any student of not only Spanish art but also the Flemish and Venetian Schools, as the collection includes the most complete representation of the work of **Bosch, Titian, El Greco, Velázquez** and **Goya** to be seen anywhere in the world.

One of the most remarkable aspects of the Prado is that its pictures remain in a near perfect state of preservation. This is due to the benefit of good climatic conditions, and the building's resistance to violent changes in temperature and relative humidity. The management pays great attention to the conservation of the paintings, subjecting them to a minimum of handling and cleaning with as little use of chemicals as possible, so that they remain remarkably free from deterioration and in a condition close to that of their creation.

Although the Prado is essentially a gallery of paintings, its other acquisitions should not be overlooked. The museum contains over 500 pieces of sculpture and a remarkable collection of medals. The Dauphin's Treasure is fascinating and includes one of the most valuable collections in the world of vases of the late Renaissance as well as some beautiful jewellery. The Prado owns some excellent pieces of furniture as well as tapestries and ceramics.

This book, however, concentrates on reproducing a selection from the many art masterpieces of the Prado. The excellence of the reproductions and the informative text make for a valuable memento for those fortunate enough to have seen the collection as well as for those interested in fine paintings who may not have the opportunity of seeing the originals.

*Left* 'Madonna and Child' by Luis de **Morales** (c. 1500-1586), a famous painter of the Spanish Renaissance who, due to the deep religious feeling, delicacy of colour and mysticism of his paintings, came to be known as 'The Divine'.

# Art Masterpieces of
# THE PRADO

## Designed and Produced by

## TED SMART

## and

## DAVID GIBBON

COLOUR LIBRARY INTERNATIONAL